flavouring with
Ginger

flavouring with

Ginger

Clare Gordon-Smith

photography by

James Merrell

RYLAND
PETERS
& SMALL

Art Director **Jacqui Small**

Art Editor **Penny Stock**

Designer **Megan Smith**

Editor **Elsa Petersen-Schepelern**

Photography **James Merrell**

Food Stylist **Clare Gordon-Smith**

Stylist **Sue Parker**

Production Manager **Kate Mackillop**

My thanks to my family – my father, sister and grandmother – to David Hurcomb, Sarah Kidd, Annabel Ford, Di Reeds, Rosemary Scoular and Vanessa Kearns, James Merrell, Sue Parker and the team at Ryland Peters & Small.

First published in Great Britain in 1998
by Ryland Peters & Small
Cavendish House, 51-55 Mortimer Street, London W1N 7TD

Text © Clare Gordon-Smith 1998
Design and photographs © Ryland Peters & Small 1998

Printed and bound in Hong Kong

ISBN 1 900518 36 8

A CIP record for this book is available from the British Library

Notes:
Ovens should be preheated to the specified temperature – if using a fan-assisted oven, adjust time and temperature according to the manufacturer's instructions.

The recipe for Tomato Chilli Jam on page 44 is reprinted with permission from Peter Gordon, author of *The Sugar Club Cookbook*, **published by Hodder & Stoughton, 1997.**

Ginger is one of the most ancient of all flavourings, used in the early civilizations of China and India, and by the Romans. The Spanish took it to the West Indies, and the Portuguese to West Africa, while in modern times it is used in one form or another in almost every cuisine. Ginger is available in several forms; **fresh root ginger** is usually peeled then sliced or grated (add a dash of lemon juice or vinegar to stop it browning). Before the advent of refrigeration and fast transport, many ways were found to keep this valuable spice – **preserved stem ginger** in sugar syrup, **crystallized ginger**, **dried ginger**, pink Japanese **pickled ginger** preserved in vinegar, or dried **ground ginger** (Jamaican ground ginger is thought to be the best). **Ginger wine**, similar to sherry, is wonderful in sauces and to give just a hint of flavour. Two botanical 'cousins' of ginger, **galangal** (second from right), and **krachai** (second from left), also known as 'Chinese keys', are both available fresh, dried or ground, and have a brighter, sharper, aromatic flavour, and are widely used in South-east Asian cooking.

ginger wine

krachai

Japanese pickled ginger

chopped dried ginger

the flavours of
Ginger

galangal

fresh root ginger

crystallized ginger

ground ginger

preserved stem
ginger in syrup

oriental marinade

Thai dipping sauce

As well as appearing alone as a flavouring ingredient, ginger also stars in some famous spice mixtures, both fresh and dried. From left is a typical **oriental marinade**, consisting of soy sauce, ginger, honey and garlic – the honey helps it stick to the food. Ginger also appears in the

Chinese Trinity of flavourings, with garlic and spring onions, and in the Thai Triad, consisting of ginger, garlic and chillies. The **Thai dipping sauce** includes ginger, chillies, shallots, soft brown sugar and rice vinegar. Make **ginger vinegar** or **ginger juice** by

8 The flavours of ginger

ginger vinegar
or ginger juice

Japanese
pickled ginger

pickling spice

mixed spice

steeping sliced ginger in rice vinegar or sherry vinegar – wonderful in dressings and marinades. **Mixed spice** is used to flavour cakes, breads and puddings, includes ginger, coriander seeds and cinnamon, and may also include other spices such as cardamom and cloves.

Pickling spice is used for all kinds of savoury pickles from cornichons to chutneys. Its precise composition varies around the world, but may include ginger, cinnamon, chillies, peppercorns, bay leaf, allspice, juniper berries, fennel seeds, and mustard seeds, all in their dried form.

The flavours of ginger **9**

Salads

Pacific ginger salad

Pacific-Rim cooking in California, Australia, and New Zealand melds the influences of European, Latin American and Asian cuisines in the most exciting way. Scallops or crab could be used in this salad instead of the salmon and prawns. Serve it as a starter or double the quantity to make a main course.

Place the spinach in a bowl, slice the papaya and avocado, add the mooli, prawns and salmon. Mix the dressing ingredients together, and pour over the salad. Sprinkle with sesame seeds and serve.

500 g baby spinach

1 papaya,
peeled and deseeded

1 avocado,
peeled and stoned

125 g mooli (Japanese
white radish), sliced

250 g cooked prawns,
peeled

50 g smoked salmon
slices

toasted sesame seeds,
to serve

ginger dressing

3 tablespoons
soy sauce

2 tablespoons
rice vinegar

1 tablespoon
sunflower oil

1 garlic clove, crushed

1–2 tablespoons
pickled ginger

Serves 4

Citus carrot salad
with ginger dressing

Carrot and orange is a favourite combination in many cuisines, but a little dash of ginger in the dressing gives this salad a subtle oriental twist that is very refreshing. It's a great salad to serve with jacket potatoes or a creamy-cheese pasta. Watercress will give a peppery edge to the salad, but you could substitute other green salad leaves.

To prepare the dressing, mix all the ingredients until thoroughly combined, then set aside. Place the watercress in a salad bowl, arrange the grated carrots and orange segments on top, pour over the dressing and serve.

about 50 g watercress

500 g young carrots, grated

3 oranges, peeled and segmented

ginger dressing

50 ml ginger vinegar (see page 8–9) or 2.5 cm fresh ginger, grated, mixed with 50 ml white rice vinegar

½ teaspoon wholegrain mustard

1 teaspoon honey

grated rind and juice of 1 medium orange

3 tablespoons olive oil

2 tablespoons toasted sesame seeds

sea salt and freshly ground black pepper

Serves 4

a fresh summer salad with a

spicy oriental twist to the dressing

Ginger chicken salad
with ogen melon and celery

Melon and ginger is a classic combination –
and a wonderful, refreshing addition to this
traditional chicken salad.

2 tablespoons olive oil

2 celery stalks,
finely chopped

2 shallots,
roughly chopped

½ teaspoon
cayenne pepper

1 ogen or
honeydew melon

1 free-range chicken,
cooked

4 tablespoons
homemade mayonnaise

6 tablespoons
soured cream

6 pieces crystallized
ginger, chopped

green salad leaves,
such as rocket and
herbs, to serve

Serves 4

Heat the olive oil in a pan, then add the celery and
shallots and gently sauté until soft. Stir in the
cayenne pepper. Let cool, then chill.
Cut the melon in half, remove and discard the seeds
and cut the flesh into cubes with a knife, or into balls
using a melon-baller or teaspoon. (Hold the melon
over a bowl to catch the juice.)
Shred the chicken into bite-sized pieces and place in
a bowl. Add the melon, celery and shallots, then stir
in the mayonnaise, soured cream and ginger.
Place the leaves on a salad platter, spoon on the
chicken, sprinkle with chopped herbs and serve.

Summer salad
with chilli and ginger dressing

Change the ingredients in this salad
according to what's fresh and exciting in the
shops. Use chicken, turkey or beef, and
leaves iike baby spinach or lambs' lettuce.
Marinate the chicken for as long as you have
available, from 30 minutes to overnight.
Chinese chives are sold in Asian markets,
but if you can't find them, use ordinary
chives or parsley instead.

Toast the cashew nuts in a dry frying pan until lightly
golden. Transfer to a small bowl and set aside.
To make the marinade, grate the zest of the orange
and squeeze the juice into a bowl. Stir in the
remaining marinade ingredients, add the chicken and
turn to coat. Marinate for 1 hour or overnight.
Mix the dressing ingredients together and set aside.
Shred the spinach and radicchio leaves and put in a
bowl. Slice the shiitakes, if using, and spring onions
and add to the bowl together with the watercress,
basil, snipped Chinese chives and toasted cashew
nuts, then transfer to a salad bowl.
Heat the oil in a frying pan, remove the chicken from
the marinade, drain (reserving the marinade), then
gently sauté the chicken until cooked – about
4 minutes. Stir in the marinade ingredients and
simmer for a few minutes. Arrange the chicken over
the salad leaves, pour over the dressing and
lukewarm marinade, then serve.

50 g cashew nuts

375 g chicken, trimmed and cut in 5 cm strips

vegetable oil, for frying

250 g young spinach

250 g radicchio

250 g fresh shiitake mushrooms (optional)

8 spring onions

a bunch of watercress

12 basil leaves

50 g Chinese chives

chilli marinade

1 orange

3 tablespoons soy sauce

1 tablespoon sugar

4 tablespoons chilli oil

ginger dressing

3 tablespoons chilli oil

3 tablespoons sherry

2 tablespoons ginger vinegar (page 8)

1 tablespoon corn oil

Serves 4

Starters

Herbed duck rolls
with ginger and plum sauce

A spectacular starter for an informal supper party. Either assemble the rolls for your guests, or set out the prepared ingredients and let them make their own parcels.

To make the crêpes, sieve the flour and salt into a bowl and make a well in the centre. Drop the eggs into the well and beat well. Gradually whisk in enough milk to make the mixture smooth and creamy. Stir in the chives and let stand for about 10 minutes. For the filling, prick the duck breasts with a fork, brush the skin with honey, sprinkle with ginger and soy sauce, then cook in a preheated oven at 190°C (375°F) Gas Mark 5 for 15–20 minutes. Heat a crêpe pan or small frying pan, brush with a little melted butter, then add a ladle of batter, rotating the pan so the base is coated with a thin layer. Cook until the underside is golden brown, loosen the edges, flip with a palette knife and cook until the other side is golden. Repeat with the remaining batter until you have 8–10 crêpes. Stack them as you go, placing a layer of greaseproof paper between each and keeping them warm in a low oven. To serve, slice the duck breast crossways. Spread a spoonful of hoisin sauce on each crêpe, add some cucumber, spring onion and a couple of slices of duck on each. Fold the crêpes into a parcel and tie up each one with a chive. Serve with soy sauce.

2 duck breasts

2 tablespoons honey

2.5 cm fresh root ginger, peeled and grated

2 teaspoons soy sauce

25–50 g melted butter

½ cucumber, cut into strips lengthways

8 spring onions, sliced lengthways

2 tablespoons hoisin sauce

a bunch of chives

soy sauce, to serve

herbed crêpes

125 g plain flour

a pinch of salt

2 eggs

150–200 ml milk

2 tablespoons chopped fresh chives

Serves 4

Seafood noodle soup

For a light ginger flavour, peel the fresh root ginger, grate it and infuse in the stock. For a stronger flavour, infuse the peel as well. Galangal or krachai could be used instead of the ginger to give a subtly different flavour.

Peel and slice the ginger, reserving the peel if preferred. Pour the stock into a large saucepan and bring to the boil. Add the soy sauce, fish sauce, sugar, lemongrass, sliced ginger and peel (optional) and simmer gently for 10–20 minutes to develop the flavours. Strain into a bowl then return to the rinsed pan. Bring to just below boiling point, add the fish and seafood, then simmer for 8 minutes more, or until the fish is just cooked and the prawns turn pink. Break the trout fillets into large pieces, add the noodles, return to the boil, then serve in small Chinese-style bowls, sprinkled with sliced spring onions and sprigs of coriander.

2.5 cm fresh ginger, peeled and sliced

500 ml chicken stock

3 tablespoons light soy sauce

1 tablespoon Thai fish sauce

½ stalk of lemongrass, lightly crushed

2 teaspoons soft brown sugar or palm sugar

400 g trout fillets

8 uncooked prawns, peeled and deveined

150 g crab meat (optional)

1 sheet Chinese rice noodles

to serve

3 spring onions, sliced diagonally

sprigs of coriander

Serves 4

ginger, galangal or krachai – all used in

Thai cooking – give **subtly different tastes**

Ginger tomato soup
with garlic and cayenne pepper

Tomato soup made with ginger and cayenne
has more 'kick' than one made with herbs.
Use good, ripe, red tomatoes – I find vine-
ripened ones have the best flavour. If serving
this soup to vegetarians, use vegetable stock
instead of chicken, but whichever kind you
use, always try to find the real thing, rather
than using cubes – these days, even
supermarkets sell real stock in plastic tubs.

Peel the tomatoes by plunging them in boiling water
for 1 minute, then slip off the skins and discard.
Coarsely chop the flesh.
Heat the oil in a saucepan, add the onion and gently
sauté until soft and translucent. Add the tomatoes,
garlic, ginger, sugar, cayenne, salt, pepper and
stock. Bring to the boil and simmer for 20 minutes
until just tender.
Serve, sprinkled with sprigs of rosemary.

Variation:
If you prefer a smooth soup, purée in a blender or
food processor before serving, though I prefer the
coarser, more homemade look of the original soup.

500 g plum tomatoes

2 tablespoons olive oil

1 onion, finely chopped

1 garlic clove, crushed

2.5 cm fresh root
ginger, grated

600 ml vegetable or
chicken stock

a pinch of brown sugar

a pinch of
cayenne pepper

sea salt and freshly
ground black pepper

sprigs of rosemary,
to serve

Serves 4

Carrot and ginger pots

Another great combination of ginger and carrots – these delicate little pots make a light summer dish, and can be made in advance. When buying ricotta cheese, always make sure it is very fresh. Sourdough bread and a crisp green salad would make suitable accompaniments.

Roughly chop the almonds and set aside, finely grate the carrots. Break the ricotta into a bowl and beat in the other ingredients to form a smooth mixture. Season, then spoon into ramekin dishes. Put the dishes into a bain-marie and cook in a preheated oven at 180°C (350°F) Gas Mark 4 for 40 minutes until just set and firm. Serve warm or chilled.

50 g almonds, blanched and skins removed

250 g young carrots

250 g ricotta cheese

1 egg, beaten

2.5 cm fresh root ginger, peeled and grated

1 tablespoon chopped fresh parsley

1 tablespoon olive oil

sea salt and freshly ground black pepper

Serves 4

Melon with ginger

A modern update of an old-fashioned dish.

Scoop out the melon flesh with a melon baller or small teaspoon. Divide between small individual glasses or place in one large glass bowl. Remove the orange peel with a zester and blanch the peel in boiling water for 2 minutes. Drain. Using a serrated knife, segment the oranges, discarding the pith. Add the orange and ginger to the melon. Sprinkle with a little sugar and orange zest and serve.

1 ogen or honeydew melon, halved and deseeded

2 medium oranges

125 g crystallized ginger, chopped

icing sugar, to taste

Serves 4

Main courses

Roasted ginger salmon
with pak choi and tabbouleh salad

This must be the ultimate in Fusion Food! Tabbouleh salad comes from the Middle East, but has Thai flavourings, while the salmon is roasted with Chinese ingredients. The result is absolutely delectable! Pak choi is now widely available, and is sometimes also sold in supermarkets as 'bok choy'.

Place the salmon pieces in a roasting tin. Brush with the lemon juice, sprinkle with salt, chilli powder and ginger and roast in a preheated oven at 200°C (400°F) Gas Mark 6 for 5 minutes.
To make the tabbouleh salad, place the couscous in a bowl, pour over 300 ml boiling water, stir in the fish sauce and let soak for 10 minutes.
Finely slice the cucumber diagonally, making the pieces as long as possible. Place the spring onions, beans and cucumber in a bowl and sprinkle over the rice vinegar. Fork through the couscous.
Heat a small pan or wok, add the corn oil and, when hot, stir-fry the pak choi and Thai seven-spice for a few minutes until the leaves are slightly wilted.
To serve, spoon the tabbouleh salad onto heated plates, add the pak choi, then top with the salmon.

4 salmon fillets, cut into narrow slices

1 tablespoon lemon juice

a pinch of salt

a pinch of chilli powder

2.5 cm fresh root ginger, thinly sliced

4 baby pak choi

1 tablespoon corn oil

2 teaspoons Thai seven-spice

tabbouleh salad

150 g easy-cook couscous

1 tablespoon Thai fish sauce

1 cucumber, peeled and deseeded

5 spring onions, finely sliced diagonally

175 g green beans, finely sliced diagonally

2 tablespoons rice vinegar

Serves 4

Five-spice snapper
with pineapple passionfruit salsa

Chinese five-spice powder is highly aromatic, with star anise being its major component. The remaining four spices are cinnamon, cloves, szechuan pepper and fennel seed. The sweet but hot crystallized ginger in the salsa accompaniment is a fine complement to those flavours.

To prepare the topping for the fish, heat the oil in a small pan, add the onion and garlic and sauté gently for 5 minutes. Remove from the heat and stir in the five-spice, ground almonds, breadcrumbs, chopped parsley and chopped nuts.

Place the fish in a greased roasting tin, spread the mixture on top of each fillet and cook in a preheated oven at 190°C (375°F) Gas Mark 5 for 10–15 minutes. Meanwhile, to make the salsa, scoop the passionfruit flesh into a small bowl, add the pineapple and crystallized ginger, stir well and use to pack the passionfruit shells. Serve with the fish.

4 snapper fillets

2 tablespoons olive oil

1 onion, finely chopped

1 large garlic clove, chopped

2 teaspoons Chinese five-spice powder

4 tablespoons ground almonds

6 tablespoons dry white breadcrumbs

3 tablespoons chopped fresh flat-leaf parsley

75 g chopped nuts

pineapple passionfruit salsa

2 passionfruit, halved, shells reserved

125 g fresh or canned pineapple, finely chopped

4 pieces crystallized ginger, chopped

Serves 4

a modern update on a

the Antipodes – serve

Ginger-roasted chicken
with red peppers and pumpkin

A Pacific-Rim recipe – Australians and New Zealanders love baked pumpkin with their Sunday roast. And they love spicy flavours from around the world – this time ginger and jerk seasoning from the Caribbean.

Put the peppers, pumpkin, onion and chilli in a roasting tin and sprinkle with the ginger, orange zest and juice. Put the chicken on top and sprinkle with jerk seasoning.

Cook in a preheated oven at 200°C (400°F) Gas Mark 6, basting every 20 minutes, for about 1 hour or until the juices run clear when the thickest part of the thigh is pierced with a skewer.

Transfer the chicken and vegetables to a serving plate and keep them warm. Strain off the fat from the pan, pour in the stock, bring to the boil and simmer for about 10 minutes on top of the stove until reduced by half. Serve with the vegetables and boiled wild rice or a mixture of basmati and wild rice.

1 yellow pepper, halved, deseeded and cut into chunks

1 red pepper, halved, deseeded and cut into chunks

500 g pumpkin or butternut squash, sliced, deseeded and peeled

1 red onion, cut into wedges

1 red chilli, halved, deseeded and thinly sliced

5 cm fresh root ginger, peeled and grated

juice and grated zest of 1 orange

1 free-range chicken, about 1.5 kg

2 teaspoons jerk seasoning

300 ml chicken stock

Serves 4

raditional Sunday roast from

with **baked pumpkin**

Lemon chicken
with saffron spiced yoghurt

Top London jewellery designer Dinny Hall
is also a brilliant cook. She showed me this
recipe for a story I did for *Marie Claire* about
designers who entertained at home. We
found that many fashion designers are
passionately interested in food and cooking.
If you don't have a chicken brick, use any
large, ovenproof casserole dish.

Put the lemon and orange inside the chicken. Make
small cuts in the chicken skin with a sharp knife and
insert the garlic and ginger slices. Place the chicken
in a soaked chicken brick and sprinkle with paprika.
Pour the yoghurt into a bowl and add the saffron, salt
and olive oil. With a mortar and pestle, crush the
coriander seeds, the black seeds from the cardamom
pods and the green peppercorns, then stir into the
yoghurt. Pour the yoghurt mixture over the chicken,
put the lid on the brick and place in a cold oven.
Turn the heat to 200°C (400°F) Gas Mark 6 and
cook for about 1½–2 hours or until the chicken
is tender. Serve with rice or vegetables.

a spicy chicken variation on

traditional **roast lamb** spiked with garlic

1 lemon, peeled

½ orange, peeled

1 free-range chicken,
about 1.5 kg

1 garlic clove, sliced

2.5 cm fresh root
ginger, peeled and
sliced

a pinch of paprika

200 ml plain yoghurt

a good pinch
of saffron threads

a pinch of salt

2 tablespoons
light olive oil

1 heaped teaspoon
coriander seeds

3 heaped teaspoons
green cardamom pods

1 teaspoon green
peppercorns

Serves 4

Barbecued chicken
on a ciabatta salad sandwich

This is a quick and easy but very flavourful recipe for roast chicken pieces. Serve it with vegetables or salad as a main course for lunch or a simple dinner – or as a filling for a special sandwich, as here.

4 free-range chicken pieces

ginger marinade

8 tablespoons tomato ketchup

2 tablespoons red wine vinegar

2.5 cm fresh root ginger, peeled and grated

1 garlic clove, crushed

to serve

1 loaf ciabatta bread

butter

salad leaves

2 ripe red Italian plum tomatoes, sliced

salt and pepper

Serves 4

Mix the marinade ingredients in a shallow dish, add the chicken, turn to coat well and set aside in the refrigerator for up to 1 hour. Remove the chicken from the marinade and char-grill on both sides until tender. Alternatively, place the chicken in a roasting tin and bake in a preheated oven at 200°C (400°F) Gas Mark 6 for 10–15 minutes until just cooked. Remove from the oven or grill and slice on a board, discarding the bones if any. To serve as a sandwich, cut the ciabatta in half lengthways, butter lightly, fill with salad leaves, sliced tomatoes and the chicken, season and serve.

Stir-fried ginger beef
with noodles and oriental vegetables

Many classic Chinese stir-fry dishes begin by
sautéing the Chinese Trinity of flavourings;
spring onions, ginger and garlic. This one
omits the garlic, and uses the ginger in the
dressing rather than the stir-fry. It's a novel
twist on a traditional combination.

First, prepare carrot curls by pulling a vegetable
peeler down the length of the carrot. Arrange them in
curls and leave for a few minutes in iced water.
Cut the sugarsnap peas in half diagonally.
Cut the spring onions diagonally into 1 cm slices.
To make the sesame dressing, mix all the ingredients
together in a small bowl.
Place the noodles in a second bowl, pour over
boiling water, let soak for a few minutes, then drain.
Heat the vegetable oil in a pan or wok, add the strips
of beef and stir-fry for about 2 minutes. Add the
vegetables and stir-fry for 5 minutes more.
Sprinkle with the sesame dressing and serve
immediately with the noodles.

2 carrots

50 g sugarsnap peas,
topped and tailed

a bunch of
spring onions

250 g Chinese
egg noodles

1 tablespoon
vegetable oil

500 g beef fillet,
cut into strips about
2.5 cm x 5 mm

sesame dressing

2.5 cm fresh root
ginger, peeled and
finely shredded

2 tablespoons
light soy sauce

1 tablespoon
rice wine vinegar

2 teaspoons chilli oil

2 tablespoons
sesame seeds

Serves 4

a quick and easy stir-fry – perfect served

with steamed rice or **Chinese noodles**

Gingered pork fillets
with a ginger apple sauce

Pork and apple is a traditional combination, and popular even with people who don't much like meat served with fruit. This apple sauce is also wonderful with venison or duck.

To make the marinade, mix the honey in a bowl with the white wine vinegar, soy sauce and grated fresh ginger. Stir well.

Slice the pork fillets diagonally, add to the marinade, turn to coat, cover and refrigerate for at least 4 hours or overnight.

Put 2 tablespoons cold water and half the caster sugar into a saucepan and cook, stirring, over a low heat until the sugar is dissolved.

Add the apple, sherry, ground ginger, salt and pepper, then cover and stew gently until just tender.

Transfer the sliced pork to a roasting tin and add 2 tablespoons cold water. Roast in a preheated oven at 200°C (400°F) Gas Mark 6 for 15–20 minutes until just tender, then transfer to a heated serving dish together with the apples.

Blanch the Chinese egg noodles in boiling water for 1 minute, or according to the packet instructions, then drain, toss in a little sesame oil, and serve with the pork and apples.

1 kg pork fillets

100 g caster sugar

500 g apples, peeled and sliced

1 tablespoon sherry

a pinch of ground ginger

salt and freshly ground black pepper

ginger marinade

3 tablespoons clear honey

2 tablespoons white wine vinegar

1 tablespoon soy sauce

2 teaspoons grated fresh root ginger

to serve

Chinese egg noodles

sesame oil

Serves 4

Mango pork kebabs
in orange and ginger marinade

Grilled or barbecued kebabs make a great
quick and easy dish, packed with zippy
flavour from the ginger marinade – and
marinated meats are always wonderful on the
barbecue. Serve with a spicy rice salad and
peppery watercress dressed with vinaigrette.

Mix the marinade ingredients in a shallow dish.
Add the pork strips to the marinade, turn to coat
well, then marinate in the refrigerator for 1–2 hours.
To assemble the kebabs, thread the pork, mango and
onions onto pre-soaked bamboo kebab sticks.
Cook under a preheated grill for about 10 minutes
turning several times, then serve immediately.

750 g pork tenderloin,
sliced crossways
into 1 cm strips

2 mangoes, sliced

4 red onions, sliced

sea salt and freshly
ground black pepper

**orange and
ginger marinade**

1 teaspoon
ground cumin

150 ml orange juice

1 teaspoon orange zest

125 ml olive oil

1 teaspoon lime zest

2 tablespoons freshly
squeezed lime juice

1 shallot, chopped

2.5 cm fresh root
ginger, grated

a small bunch of
fresh coriander leaves

Serves 4

this **ginger-orange marinade** tenderizes

the pork while infusing it with **flavour**

Accompaniments

Ginger apple chutney

Chutneys are the wonderful spicy savoury
preserves that the British found in India and
enthusiastically adopted as their own.
Chutneys taste particularly good with cold
meats and cheese, and contain various
amounts of spices, both aromatic and hot.
This one is spicy, but not overly so.

Put the apples in a non-aluminium pan with the
treacle and 300 ml of the vinegar. Cook over a
medium heat until thick and pulpy.
Stir in the remaining vinegar, followed by the sugar,
ginger, mixed spice, cayenne, salt, pepper and
raisins. Cook for a further 5 minutes, or until thick.
Bottle in sterilized jars. Cover and label.

1.75 kg Bramley
cooking apples, peeled,
cored and chopped

1 tablespoon treacle

500 ml cider vinegar

500 g soft brown sugar

2.5 cm fresh root
ginger, chopped

a pinch of mixed spice

a pinch of
cayenne pepper

½ teaspoon salt

black and white pepper

500 g seedless raisins

**Makes 3 jars
of 500 ml**

Tomato chilli jam

This chilli jam is a signature dish from one of London's most innovative chefs – New Zealander Peter Gordon of the Sugar Club Restaurant in the more raffish end of fashionable Notting Hill. This is a great relish to keep in the fridge, and good with chicken, fish and pork, or spread on toast with goats' cheese and rocket leaves.

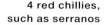

4 red chillies, such as serranos

4 garlic cloves

2.5 cm fresh root ginger, peeled and roughly chopped

50 ml Thai fish sauce

500 g very ripe red cherry tomatoes

300 g golden caster sugar

100 ml red wine vinegar

Makes 3 jars of 250 ml

Put the chillies, garlic, ginger, fish sauce and half the tomatoes in a blender and whizz to a fine purée. Cut the remaining tomatoes into 5 mm dice and set aside. Place the purée, sugar and vinegar into a deep saucepan and bring gently to the boil, stirring constantly. When it reaches boiling point, reduce to a gentle simmer, add the diced tomatoes and skim off any foam that rises to the surface. Cook for about 30–45 minutes, stirring from time to time to release the solids that settle on the base. Scrape the sides of the pot during cooking. Pour the jam into warmed, sterilized glass jars and let cool to room temperature. Seal with lids and store in the refrigerator. Use within 1 month.

Rhubarb ginger jam

Rhubarb and ginger is a classic combination, and if forced rhubarb is in season, this delicate jam will be a very pretty pink.

3 kg rhubarb, cut into 5 cm lengths

rind and juice of 2 lemons

150 g fresh root ginger, lightly crushed

3 kg sugar

Makes 4 jars of 1 litre

Put the rhubarb in a preserving pan. Tie up the lemon rind and crushed ginger in muslin and add to the pan. Bring slowly to the boil, then simmer until tender (about 8 minutes), stirring as necessary. Stir in the lemon juice and sugar until dissolved, then boil for about 10 minutes. To test for setting, put 1 teaspoon jam on a cold saucer. Wait for 5 minutes, then push with your finger. If the surface wrinkles, the jam is set. If not, boil a few minutes longer. Pour into sterilized jars, seal and use within 4 months.

Cranberry conserve
with apples and ginger

A sweet and sour, spicy and savoury accompaniment for game or poultry.

500 g apples, peeled, cored and diced

1 tablespoon golden granulated sugar

250 ml maple syrup

500 g cranberries

grated zest of 1 orange

2.5 cm fresh root ginger, grated

Makes 4 jars of about 300 ml

Put the apples, sugar and 2 tablespoons water in a pan and shake to stop the apples sticking. Mix in the maple syrup, cranberries, orange zest and ginger and cook at a high heat. When the berries begin to burst, reduce the heat to low, cover, stir occasionally and cook for 10 minutes. Pour into sterilized jars, then seal and use within 4 months.

Puddings

Plum berry compote
with lime leaves and ginger

A compote is a gentle stew of fresh fruits,
served alone or with cream or ice cream. Use
single fruits, or a combination or fruits – this
one uses all-red varieties. The subtle ginger
syrup gives it a spicy bright taste.

Halve and stone the plums, trim and cut the rhubarb
into 2.5 cm pieces, and pick over the raspberries.
Put the sugar and water in a saucepan, heat gently
to dissolve the sugar, then bring to the boil and
simmer for 5 minutes.
Add the lime leaves, if using, then stir in the ginger
and ginger wine and allow to infuse for 30 minutes.
Stir in the fruit and simmer for 7–10 minutes until the
fruit is just soft but still holds its shape. Remove the
lime leaves and serve with crème fraîche and biscuits
such as the Ginger Shortbread on page 62.

500 g plums

500 g rhubarb

250 g raspberries

125 g caster sugar

125 ml water

3 kaffir lime leaves
(optional)

50 g preserved
stem ginger, chopped

3 tablespoons ginger
wine (or 1 tablespoon
sherry mixed with
2 tablespoons orange
juice and 1 teaspoon
grated ginger)

Serves 4

Steamed puddings
with ginger and apricot

Steamed puddings are the perfect comfort food, and you can make them with any number of variations. I often cook them in ovenproof cups or moulds which look very pretty, though you can also make a large one. When made in small dariole moulds, they are called Castle Puddings.

To make the topping, melt the butter in a small pan, stir in the sugar and honey and heat until dissolved. Divide the apricot halves between 6 well-buttered ramekin dishes, teacups, moulds or a 1 litre pudding basin. Arrange them, curved side down, then spoon in the melted topping mixture.

To make the sponge, cream the butter and sugar until soft and creamy. Gradually beat in the eggs, then fold in the flour, ginger and crystallized ginger. Spoon on top of the apricots, then cover each dish with a piece of greaseproof paper a little larger than the mould. Secure with string.

Place in large pan of boiling water so the water comes half way up the sides of the moulds, then simmer for about 1 hour.

Serve with a vanilla custard.

apricot topping

50 g unsalted butter

50 g soft brown sugar

2 tablespoons honey

300 g canned apricot
halves, drained

ginger sponge

125 g unsalted butter,
softened

125 g caster sugar

2 eggs

125 g self-raising flour

1 teaspoon
ground ginger

75 g crystallized
ginger, chopped

Serves 4

Ginger bavarois
with honey and chocolate

Bavarois make very classic and elegant puddings. Though simple, they need a little patience to make, but are always worth the trouble. Whipped cream is folded into a traditional custard, which is then set with gelatine. Leaf gelatine is now widely available and I find it much easier to use.

Place the milk and almonds in a pan and bring to just below boiling point. Remove from the heat, stir in the ginger wine and leave to infuse for 10 minutes. Whisk the egg yolks until light and fluffy (about 3–4 minutes). Stir in the hot milk and honey. Return the custard to the pan and heat gently, stirring, until thickened – do not allow to boil or the mixture will curdle.

Dissolve the gelatine according to the packet instructions. Fold the gelatine into the custard, fill a bowl with ice and set the pan of custard on top. Whisk the custard until almost set. Lightly whip the cream and fold into the custard. Pour the mixture into 6 small moulds or 1 large one and leave to set in the refrigerator for a few hours.

To serve, gently melt the chocolate over a pan of simmering water. Invert the moulds onto individual serving plates, spoon some single cream around the bavarois. Drizzle the melted chocolate over the pudding and sprinkle with toasted flaked almonds and preserved ginger.

350 ml full-cream milk

100 g whole almonds, coarsely chopped

4 tablespoons ginger wine

4 egg yolks

50 g caster sugar

2 tablespoons honey

5 sheets gelatine

200 ml double cream

to decorate

50 g plain chocolate, melted

25 g flaked almonds, toasted

50 g preserved stem ginger, cut into pieces

Serves 4

Gingered berry tarts

Crystallizing is one of the oldest forms of preserving ginger, and is therefore found in many traditional recipes, especially for treats such as puddings and cakes.

To make the pastry, mix the flour and sugar in a bowl, then rub in the butter until it resembles breadcrumbs. Fold in the egg yolks and just enough water to bind the mixture (about 1–2 teaspoons). Wrap the pastry in clingfilm or foil and chill for about 30 minutes.

Roll out the pastry on a floured surface and use to line eight 10 cm loose-based flan tins. Trim the edges, then chill for 30 minutes. Line the pastry with foil or baking parchment and fill with dried beans or ceramic baking beans. Cook in a preheated oven at 200°C (400°F) Gas Mark 6 for 10–15 minutes until lightly browned at the edges. Remove from the oven and remove the baking parchment and beans.

To make the pastry cream, beat the eggs, egg yolks and sugar in a bowl. In another bowl, beat the cornstarch and milk until smooth, beat in the cream, then beat into the egg mixture.

Bring gently to the boil on top of the stove, then turn down the heat and cook, stirring, until thickened. Let cool, then spoon into the pastry cases, top with the fruit and ginger and serve.

175 g plain flour, sieved

50 g caster sugar

75 g unsalted butter

2 egg yolks

a little iced water

pastry cream

2 eggs

2 egg yolks

50 g caster sugar

2 tablespoons cornflour

175 ml warm milk

300 ml double cream

to decorate

125 g blueberries
or wild strawberries

125 g raspberries
or pitted cherries

6 pieces crystallized
or preserved ginger,
sliced

Serves 4

Gingered tea granita

A granita is a frozen liquid, mashed into
small pieces before serving. It is softer than
a sorbet, but not as smooth. This is a frozen
version of Chinese ginger tea, often served
at the end of a meal to aid digestion – in fact
ginger tea is well-known throughout Asia as
a good way to soothe an upset stomach.

600 ml water

300 g sugar

5 cm fresh root ginger,
peeled and sliced

zest and juice of
1 lemon

Serves 4

Put the water and sugar in a saucepan and heat
gently until the sugar has dissolved. Simmer gently
for 3 minutes.
Add the ginger, lemon zest and juice to the
simmering water and leave to infuse for 20 minutes.
Strain and serve as tea, or cool and freeze. To serve,
allow to thaw a little for about 15–30 minutes, then
scoop into serving dishes with a small teaspoon.

a soft sorbet with a thrilling
zippy edge to its **icy, spicy flavour**

Ginger ice cream
with crystallized ginger and cherries

Ginger is the perfect ingredient for ices and ice creams. Cold dulls flavour, but the strength of ginger is robust enough to survive the freezing process.

Place the milk and ground ginger in a heavy-based saucepan and heat to simmering point. Beat the egg yolks and sugar together in a large mixing bowl until thick and pale yellow in colour (about 3–4 minutes). Gradually pour the hot milk into the egg mixture, stirring all the time.

Strain the mixture into a heavy-based or double saucepan and stir over a gentle heat until the custard thickens enough to coat the back of a wooden spoon. Do not allow to boil.

Pour into a large mixing bowl and let cool.

Beat the cream until it forms soft peaks then fold into the custard. Pour into a freezer container and freeze for about 1 hour.

Stir the crystallized ginger and glacé cherries into the ice cream and return it to the freezer for 1 hour more. Beat, cover, seal and freeze.

If using an ice cream maker, do not beat the cream, but stir into the egg mixture just before churning. Churn, stir in the ginger and cherries, then serve immediately or freeze.

If frozen hard, transfer to the refrigerator for about 20 minutes before serving.

450 ml full-cream milk

1 teaspoon ground ginger

4 egg yolks

75 g caster sugar

150 ml double or whipping cream

75 g crystallized or stem ginger, finely chopped

25 g glacé cherries, (optional)

Serves 4

creamy, spicy

ice cream

tastes in this sumptuous

form the **perfect finale** for a great dinner

Baking

Gingerbread

Gingerbread has been popular for centuries and is thought to have been introduced to Europe at the time of the Crusades. It is a very easy recipe – all the liquid ingredients are heated in a pan, then the dry ingredients are added, followed by the beaten egg. Serve it plain, or drizzle over the light lemon glaze used in the following recipe.

125 g butter

125 g soft brown sugar

125 g black treacle

125 g golden syrup

150 ml full-cream milk

250 g plain flour

3–4 teaspoons ground ginger

1 teaspoon bicarbonate of soda

1 large egg, beaten

Makes 16

Grease and line a 20 cm square cake tin. Melt the butter, sugar, treacle, syrup and milk in a saucepan over a low heat, stirring all the time. Remove from the heat and cool until lukewarm. Sieve the dry ingredients and stir into the liquid. Beat in the beaten egg, mixing until smooth, then spoon the mixture into the prepared tin. Bake in a preheated oven at 150°C (300°F) Gas Mark 2 for 1¼–1½ hours until cooked, or when a cocktail stick is inserted and comes out clean. Cool for 5 minutes on a wire rack, then turn out of the tin onto the rack and cool completely. Cut into 16 pieces and serve immediately, or transfer to an airtight tin and eat within 1 week.

Ginger cake

This wonderful, old-fashioned cake recipe was found in a very old cookbook. It's the kind of cake our grannies used to make – tried and tested, by people who really knew the secret of successful baking!

Grease and line a 23 cm deep ring mould. Cream the butter and sugar together (about 10 minutes), then gradually beat in the eggs. Coarsely chop the cherries, ginger and pineapple and stir into the mixture. Sieve the flour, baking powder, ginger and cinnamon and stir into the mixture, adding enough of the milk to give a soft dropping consistency. Spoon into the greased mould and cook in a preheated oven at 190°C (375°F) Gas Mark 5 for about 45 minutes to 1 hour. Test by piercing the top of the cake with a cocktail stick: it is cooked when the stick comes out clean. Remove from the oven, let cool for 5 minutes, then turn out onto a wire rack to cool completely. To make the light lemon glaze, sieve the icing sugar into a bowl, then stir in the lemon juice and boiling water until the mixture is quite runny. Using a teaspoon, drizzle the mixture over the cake. Decorate with crystallized ginger pieces and glacé cherries and serve immediately, or transfer to an airtight container. The cake will keep for up to 1 week, or can be frozen for up to 1 month.

an easy

old-fashioned cake recipe

just like **grannie used to make**

150 g unsalted butter

150 g caster sugar

2 eggs

50 g glacé cherries

75 g crystallized ginger

75 g glacé pineapple

200 g plain flour

½ teaspoon
baking powder

1 teaspoon
ground ginger

¼ teaspoon
ground cinnamon

100 ml full-cream milk

light lemon glaze

125 g icing sugar

juice of 1 lemon

1–2 teaspoons
boiling water

to decorate

125 g preserved stem
ginger, sliced

125 g glacé cherries,
halved

Makes 1 cake,
23 cm diameter

Ginger shortbread
with orange and lemon zest

Everyone loves shortbread – made with cornflour or rice flour to make it especially crisp. You can cook it in a round tart tin, cut it into rounds with a biscuit cutter, shape it into a circle with your hands – or use this long slim tart tin so you can cut it crossways into biscuit bars. Ginger has always been a favourite flavouring for this classic, but you could also use all sorts of other flavourings, such as nuts and spices.

300 g plain flour

50 g cornflour or rice flour

250 g salted butter, softened

125 g golden granulated sugar

125 g crystallized ginger, roughly chopped

grated zest of 1 lemon

grated zest of 1 orange

caster sugar, for dusting

Makes 16

Grease a Swiss roll tin, or a rectangular tart tin about 36 x 12 x 2.5 cm.

Sieve the two flours together in a bowl, then rub the softened butter into the flour until it resembles fine meal. Stir in the sugar, ginger, orange and lemon zest, then knead until the mixture forms a soft dough. Place the dough in the greased tin and push out to fill the corners. Using a knife, mark the dough crossways into bars.

Bake in a preheated oven at 180°C (350°F) Gas Mark 4 for 45 minutes, until pale in colour. (It will still be soft to the touch.) Cut the shortbread crossways into bars while warm, then dust with caster sugar. When cool, turn out onto a wire rack and when cold transfer to an airtight container. The shortbread will keep for about 1 week, or freeze for up to 1 month.

Index